A GIFT OF GROWTH

FOR

_____

FROM

_____

A GIFT OF GROWTH

"GIFTS OF GROWTH"

Books Available

DETACHMENT
Seven Simple Steps

•

ENABLING

•

MY FIRST NINETY DAYS

Distributed by
PERRIN & TREGGETT
P.O. Box 190
Rutherford, NJ 07070
1-800-321-7912

ENABLING

by

JUDITH M. KNOWLTON
and
REBECCA D. CHAITIN

QUOTIDIAN
Delaware Water Gap
Pennsylvania, 18327

ISBN 0-934391-01-7
FIRST EDITION
3rd Printing—1987

QUOTIDIAN
1987

CONTENTS

*This is a companion book to
"Detachment: Seven Simple Steps,"
which ought to be read first.*

ENABLING

Living with alcoholism is lousy living
at best. By now you have probably put
inmense amounts of time, energy and
effort into making it tolerable. But the
painful truth is, *it hasn't worked.* And
deep down, you know it!

- 1 -

When, at long last, you swallow your pride and "go public" by seeking help in Al-Anon or private counseling, almost immediately you get a shock. You are told that everything you've been doing has been "enabling" the alcoholic to *stay sick!*

The word itself is confusing. Surely "enabling" means to help someone? Not when dealing with alcoholism! In this context, enabling means *helping to preserve, protect and maintain the addiction.*

Have you really been doing all that? And if so, how could you have failed to recognize it? It's simple. Enabling happens when you behave as you were brought up to do -- when you put up a brave front, when you work to keep a peaceful and stable home, when you try to protect everyone around you from pain and suffering -- in short, *when you are doing the very best you can!*

How do you stop enabling? Simply by *rethinking everything you've ever learned to do!*

Keep in mind that the alcoholic only does or says as much as he* needs to in order to protect his drinking -- his *addiction.* Once alcoholism takes hold, that's his first and only priority. As you look at your own behavior, quietly begin to observe what he does to maneuver you into *helping* him maintain his drinking.

Unfortunately, in our society it seems that everything conspires to help an alcoholic drink, especially in the early years, when his consumption is probably excessive but seems sufficiently "controlled" to be socially acceptable. Later on, when the drinking becomes more unpredictable -- sometimes relatively normal, sometimes totally

---

*"He" can just as easily be "she".

uncontrolled -- you keep hoping it's just a passing phase, that it will get better. Or you believe the alcoholic's (sincere) morning-after promise that "This time it's going to be different." The descent into alcoholism can be so gradual that everyone is lulled into false hope -- including the alcoholic.

But the fact is, *alcoholism is a progressive disease that only gets worse, never better.* The earlier you and others around the alcoholic learn to stop enabling, the greater the likelihood that he will come to recognize his condition and begin his recovery -- before brain damage and long-term addiction make such recognition difficult or even impossible.

Co-alcoholics (a short-cut term for those affected by an alcoholic) are motivated to enable for various compelling social and personal reasons. These reasons often appear to be good and even generous -- but in the presence of alcoholism they become twisted and misused. Let's examine some of them to see how they actually perpetuate the addiction.

NOTES

PEACE AT ANY PRICE

Trying to keep a calm home or a balanced relationship is a full-time job. It takes effort and dedication. But when alcoholism enters the picture, the pendulum of daily living swings wildly between the extremes of hyperkinetic craziness and dull, drained exhaustion. Yet every action you take to bring things back to a stable middle ground will force you into a position *contrary* to your own best interests.

If this seems paradoxical, ask yourself these questions:

- Do you find yourself shushing the children when the alcoholic makes unreasonable demands, rather than supporting the children's *reasonable* position?
- Does the threat of the alcoholic's anger send you running to do his bidding even if what he's demanding is *wrong*?
- Have you become ever more skillful at taking on extra tasks (dropping the good things you'd *really* like to be doing) just to placate him or to avoid verbal or physical abuse?

In other words, *have you betrayed your own standards and accepted the unacceptable as a trade-off for "a little peace and quiet?"*

This kind of "peace" has a high price indeed. The constant tension damages you in many subtle ways. It keeps you from paying attention to your own life, pleasures and needs. Over a long period of time, it may result in subtle inner erosion and physical symptoms such as high blood pressure, colitis, eating disorders, migraines or gynecological problems. Maybe that's the price you've unwittingly been paying. We doubt if you recognized the connection.

In children, the effects emerge as hostility, withdrawal, poor sleep or school habits, frenetic over achieving, outright anger and violence, or even ulcers. Some peace!

Enabling has yet another consequence: the alcoholic is behaving irresponsibly and unacceptably. His addiction leads him to make childishly self-centered, irrational demands -- and everyone dances to his tune! To him, it seems that things are working out just fine. In fact, the more he drinks and the more unreasonable he becomes, the more effort you put into doing it *his* way. Isn't that insane? You bet it is! The actual price of "peace at any price" is accelerated drinking and all the horrors that go with it.

THE CONSPIRACY OF SILENCE

If you are like most of us, you were taught not to wash your dirty linen in public. You were expected to protect the family image and endorse a "what will the neighbors think?" mentality. To some extent, consideration of others' opinions is necessary in any organized society, but it can be carried much too far.

Alcoholic behavior is hurtful, crude, intimidating, violent -- and acutely embarrassing. But if you say and do nothing, you allow the alcoholic to remain blissfully unaware of the effect his actions have on you. In fact, *your silence tells him that his behavior is okay!* Unless he is told that something is wrong, it is human and natural for him to assume that what he is doing is perfectly acceptable.

The need to avoid embarrasment is a potent motivator. Most of us will go to great lengths to avoid being embarrassed or embarrassing someone else. But if you allow this need to direct just one of your actions, you're on the road to full-blown enabling!

It's true that if you speak up, you'll find yourself standing uncomfortably at center stage. Does this fear keep you silent? Consider the consequences. Say you're at a party and the alcoholic has gotten drunk (what else!). You don't want to call attention to yourself by pointing out the obvious, so you slink silently into the passenger seat of the car for the drive home.

What message have you given? You have told the alcoholic: first, that he is not drunk enough to be out of control, and second, that you trust his drunk driving enough to put your *life* in his hands. *Your* motive is clear enough -- "I'd rather be dead than embarrassed" -- plus you've allowed *him* to maintain the comfortable delusion that he's in control of himself. Think about it. THAT'S CRAZY!

You must never make the mistake of assuming that he really *knows* how you feel about his drinking. No way! In this world, there are no mind-readers. If you haven't spoken up, he *doesn't* know! He's in a sedated state anyway (from the sedative drug alcohol) and YOUR SILENCE MEANS CONSENT.

The conspiracy of silence surrounding alcoholism is pervasive. It affects neighbors and friends, doctors and counselors, but especially those within the immediate family group. In fact, others may be taking their cue from *you*. If you act as if "everything-is-fine-thank-you-just-fine," how is anyone else supposed to act? If you can't bring yourself to say, "You're drunk and disgusting and I'm embarrassed," who will?

When you speak up, it's vital that you avoid a nagging, accusatory tone. Keep your statements simple and factual.* Nagging is just as harmful -- and just as tacitly consenting -- as silence, because it puts *you* in the wrong and the alcoholic in the right. "I wouldn't *need* to drink if you weren't always hammering at me!" is the kind of defensive response you can expect. Do you see how this puts the focus on *you* and off the real problem?

* For more on this, see "Detachment: Seven Simple Steps"

GETTING YOU IN
YOUR GUILT

First we learned to be good little girls
and boys. Then we took on the stereo-
types of good wives and husbands and,
later, good parents. We really have
been trying so hard to be good people!
And if anyone accuses us of *not* living
up to our own expectations, we become

terribly guilty and jump to behave as we "should". Doesn't the alcoholic know this all too well?

So this is what you'll hear from him: "If you really loved me, you would..."; "A good mother would give me the money for..."; "If there's anything I can't stand it's a nagging wife who..."; and the old standby: "Is it any *wonder* I drink?"

The overriding message in this barrage of guilt-inducing statements is: "Do it *my* way. Lay off my drinking. (That's sacrosanct.) *You're* the real problem."

But a well-honed sense of guilt doesn't even need messages from him to trigger it. All those "if only" thoughts swirl in your head anyway. You know the kind we mean: "If only I were a better parent, child, lover, cook, housekeeper, worker..." To stop that awful, sick feeling of guilt, you'll do just about *anything!*

Now you're really in a jam. The alcoholic has harnessed your guilt to maintain and protect his habit and you've got yourself believing, "I must be doing something wrong. If I can just figure out how to do it *right*, the bad alcoholic behavior will go away." Do you honestly believe that? This very thought alone can help the alcoholic to stay drunk!

Say that hubby comes home smashed and the house is a wreck. You've been to an Al-Anon meeting, a counselor and a Family Education Program this week (it's only Wednesday) and hubby's either about to pick a fight and storm out to drink or get you feeling guilty so he can drink peacefully at home.

He starts bitching about the mess and slams a little furniture around for emphasis. "You never do a thing around here," he swears...

Boy, can you feel your guilt and shame coming on! Your mind is already running through the house grabbing the vacuum, the duster, the sponge... BUT YOU CAN STOP. You can tell your guilt to bug off and zero in on the *truth.*

"Yes, you're right, the place *is* a mess. I've been going to several alcoholism programs this week. Right now that's my priority." And you smile gently and walk away.

So your guilt doesn't have to lead you by the nose. Use your brain instead. Listen to the experts, the experienced A.A. and Al-Anon members who know the twists and turns of alcoholic thinking, and your own thinking will begin to straighten out. The best rule may be: "Feel guilty if you must, but *don't act on it!*"

YOUR SENSE OF DUTY

Like guilt, this can backfire on you. You probably have a strong perception of your role and obligations as a parent, spouse, child, friend, employer or employee. You know what these roles mean to you, and when things get out of whack, your sense of duty goes into high gear. Which might be fine if you brought your mind along, but what usually happens goes something like this:

Mother or Father: You gallop off to court to pay your kid's bail (again!), or keep on paying for college even though the return is, at best, a D average!

Wife: You dress in your best to go out for an anniversary dinner with your husband, even though you know that drunkenness will be the main feature of the evening and that there is truly nothing to celebrate.

Husband: You turn down the idea of a rehab for your wife or counseling for yourself because a "good" man manages *all* his family's affairs -- in private.

Adult child: You eagerly pay your alcoholic mother's rent, thus leaving her with enough extra cash to buy liquor -- in short, subsidizing her addiction.

Supervisor: You don't make a negative report about the alcoholic to your boss, because he has been a respected employee for many years and you don't want to "hurt" him or jeopardize his job.

Your kindness and sympathy are misplaced. All of these examples are classic enabling behaviors because, in every instance, the alcoholic is given the clear message that *he doesn't have to suffer any consequences for his drinking behavior!* In fact, there *are* no consequences! Every time there's a threat of trouble, the enabler steps in -- with the best motives in the world -- to smooth things over. With no need to face up to the harsh realities, the alcoholic can sit back, relax...and keep on drinking.

NOTES

TAKING OVER
RESPONSIBILITIES

Often the motivating force behind this type of enabling is simple frustration. Jobs aren't getting done. The alcoholic is so irresponsible that you can expect nothing from him, or so sick that he's barely functioning. And you're beginning to treat him like an incapacitated child, *which fast becomes a self-ful-filling prophecy!* Some examples:

Housewife: You take over paying all the household bills. Terrific! Now the alcoholic doesn't have to deal with or even *see* the financial problems his drinking has created, and he has more time to drink in peace.

Secretary: You notice missed appointments, make calls and excuses, and reschedule meetings at earlier hours, before the martinis have set in. Certainly this will postpone the day when your boss is confronted about his poor job performance; it will also postpone any chance of recovery!

Parents: You allow your 24-year-old unemployed addict to live at home, rent-free. (But where will he *go?*, you cry!) He has no responsibilities. He's sick, all right, and doesn't have to put an ounce of effort into survival. You've taken that painful, life-sustaining job away from him!

Husband: You come home from work to find your sloshed wife passed out on the sofa. You rush around making dinner for yourself and the kids too, and polish up the kitchen while you're at it. She doesn't have to do a thing!

By all these actions, you say to the alcoholic, "You are unable to do this for yourself because you are incompetent and irresponsible; *I must do it for you.*" The alcoholic's low self-esteem slides ever lower, a negative feeling *that makes alcohol even more necessary and attractive.* And the lack of responsibility allows the drinking to be relatively comfortable and pain free. (Remember that alcoholics don't confront their addiction until it hurts -- a lot!)

NOTES

EXPLAINING IT
ALL AWAY

Reasonable people look at an alcoholic's irrational behavior and try to make some sense out of it. Ignorant of the nature of addiction, they explain it in their own rational terms. The alcoholic *must* be drinking because of:

- a poor self-image
- a stressful job

- (ten years after) the death of a child
- bad companions
- unemployment or financial problems
- a rotten marriage
- a terrible childhood

Recovering alcoholics know better. Go to an Open Speaker's meeting of Alcoholics Anonymous and you will hear a simple truth: ALCOHOLICS DRINK BECAUSE THEY ARE ALCOHOLIC! Oh yes, the excessive drinking *may* have been triggered by various problems, but the reverse is more often true: the bad companions, rotten marriage, poor self-image and financial distress are *results* of drinking, not causes. (Everyone has life traumas, but only alcoholics get drunk for *years* over them!)

Today's repetitive, obsessive and compulsive drinking stems from *today's addiction!* As A.A. members say, "There are no reasons for drinking, only excuses."

Do you see how the focus is shifting toward the alcoholic and *his* responsibility? We are not refuting alcoholism as a disease -- far from it -- but we want you to know that one of its salient characteristics is irresponsible behavior. An alcoholic does not get sober until he is *willing to*, and he must recognize his own responsibility in the process. Those who shield him from the consequences are truly enabling: *denying him a chance to recover!*

So you can stop trying to fix the unfixable -- the awful past, the stressful present -- through misplaced sympathy, psychiatry or whatever. When the alcoholic comes home late with the excuse that he "stopped off for a few drinks because of a rough day at the office," you can stop enabling him by replying gently, "No, you drank because you're hooked on alcohol and you need help to stop drinking."

Try it. It's a blast of reality. And reality is what will help get the alcoholic *into treatment to stop drinking.*

TO STOP ENABLING:
THREE THOUGHTS

First Thought:
Is It Really Helping?

We have assured you that, to stop enabling, all you have to do is *rethink everything you've ever learned to do!* That is strictly the truth, as you've probably discovered. To accomplish this difficult life-and-attitude change, it's helpful to use "mind-stoppers," those little words or signals you use silently within your head to make you pause. Any word that gets you to evaluate your actions is fine: WHOA! STOP! HOLD IT! THINK!

Before taking any action, consider the consequences for you as well as for the alcoholic. We're not just talking about crises, but simple daily interactions too. Pause for a moment -- use a "mind-stopper" if you like -- and ask yourself "Is this thing I want to do (or *not* do) really helpful?" Remember that true helpfulness is the opposite of enabling!

Check it out with the experts. Experienced "Program People" (A.A. and Al-Anon members) and alcoholism counselors can help you see the distinction between enabling and truly supportive behaviors.

Eventually your new approaches toward the alcoholic will become second nature, but not right away. You may very well feel miserable, guilty, uneasy and awkward at first when you don't rush to his rescue the way you always did before. This is normal and expected. Just keep talking with the experts!

Second Thought:
Whose Responsibility Is It?

Allowing the alcoholic to experience the full consequences of his drinking is hard. As we've said, it goes against a whole lifetime of training. So "mindstop" again, and ask yourself (and answer truthfully): "Is it MY responsibility or HIS?"

For example, he's been convicted of drunk driving and lost his license. Do you drive him to work or leave him to arrange his own transportation? To make this example more difficult (and realistic): If you drive him it's a half-hour trip, and if he takes public transportation it's an hour and a half in the rain and snow and cold. By now, you know full well what *we* think! But saying NO to the alcoholic for the first time is going to be very rough.

And you will discover soon enough that all his other "enablers" are against you; suddenly *you're* the bad guy. Friends and relatives will consider you mean. Give them this book to read (it doesn't take long). More important, keep drawing support from Program People. Your stand is a lonely one, and you'll often slip back because the new ways feel so alien.

Sometimes the only way to break enabling behavior is "cold turkey". If you've been successfully manipulated by an alcoholic for a long period, you may have to go so far as not speaking to him or even seeing him for a month or so, in order not to get sucked back in. This period will be like withdrawal -- full of guilt, anxiety and fear -- particularly if your decision to stop enabling is still half formed or without conviction.

You will need all the support you can get when the alcoholic starts putting on the pressure. And he will. For a while it's all going to get more tense and uncomfortable. Why? His experience tells him that it's only a matter of time, or finding the right combination, before he breaks you down again!

Remember, you really can't stop enabling all at once. That's expecting too much of yourself. For the first few months, everything will feel worse, and you'll be especially vulnerable. Keep up your Al-Anon meetings and listen to A.A. speakers. In time, it *will* get easier and more natural.

Third Thought:
What Are My Motives?

As you change, expect some confusion in your own mind about your motives. (ALL motives are mixed -- and we're so good at rationalizing our actions!) The praise you've gotten for "taking care" of the alcoholic -- that is, letting him get away with it -- will tempt you back to doing just that. The blame you get when you stop protecting his drinking feels terrible. It's all too comfortable to slide back into the old enabling ways -- "for his sake." But your true motive may be the need to return to misery that is at least familiar, or to martyr yourself, or to take the heat off, or to get back to that tried-and-true role of "good person."

Your "de-enabling" program can also get derailed if you become too attached to your role as the only functioning adult in the house. Usually the whole family shifts roles *around* the alcoholic -- who, of course, is no longer behaving like a grown-up -- and people adjust well to these roles. They don't like their positions challenged. This means that impending sobriety can be a *real threat* -- the unknown quantity that's going to force everyone to shift positions once again.

If you keep backsliding into taking over for the alcoholic, or controlling him, you probably *are* threatened by the idea that he might resume his adult role. It's also very tempting to hold onto your righteous anger -- but you must set it aside if you're going to become rational about this disease!

You may also find that, as you move away from enabling, something inside you gets a sneaking satisfaction from watching the alcoholic squirm. That's understandable, within limits. But if you get into power-tripping him (playing on vulnerability), there's a danger that you'll lose sight of your original goal: *creating a climate in which sobriety becomes possible.*

Back to the experts again when you're unsure of your motives. As you struggle to understand what really prompts your actions, their smiles of recognition will help. You know instinctively that they've been there -- they're not laughing *at* you, but *with* you.

"Let go," they'll probably tell you; "Let him hurt". And that may be the best advice you will ever get.

It is true that the alcoholic cannot accept help until he "hits bottom." And once you slip your fluffy cushion of support out from under him, he'll *notice* the next fall. This is the painful step YOU must take to help him on the road to sobriety. Whether or not he welcomes that new life will depend upon HIM.

NOTES

SYMPTOMS OF ALCOHOLISM

DOES THE ALCOHOLIC:

1. have a personality change when drinking?
2. suffer memory lapses?
3. have problems at home, at work or socially because of drinking behavior?
4. cover up or protect drinking?
5. drink more before becoming intoxicated?
6. drink *less* before becoming intoxicated?

IS THE ALCOHOLIC:

7. making mistakes or having accidents (physical, auto, or mechanical) because of drinking?
8. losing time from duties or responsibilities?
9. angry and defensive about drinking?
10. sneaking or gulping drinks?
11. hiding bottles or cans?

OR IS IT THAT:

12. the drinking is bothering YOU?

For an Up to Date
Catalog of Books
on All Aspects
of Alcoholism

THOMAS W. PERRIN, INC.
Post Office Box 190
Rutherford, New Jersey 07070

SUGGESTED READING

AL-ANON'S TWELVE AND TWELVE
Al-Anon Family Groups, Inc.,
New York City, 1983

ALCOHOLICS ANONYMOUS
(A.A.'s "Big Book")
Alcoholics Anonymous,
New York City, 1976

THE ART OF SELFISHNESS
David Seabury: Pocket Books, 1964

THE BOOZE BATTLE
Ruth Maxwell: Ballantine Books, 1976

GETTING THEM SOBER
(Volumes I, II & Action Guide)
Toby Rice Drews:
Bridge Publishing, 1980

NEW PRIMER ON ALCOHOLISM
Marty Mann: Holt, Rinehart
& Winston, 1972

NOTES

JUDITH M. KNOWLTON

Judy has a degree in Psychology from Oberlin College and her Master's in Group Process from Seton Hall University. A recovering alcoholic, she is a Certified Alcoholism Counselor with ten years' experience. Judy has been instrumental in starting several alcoholism programs in northern New Jersey. She is the founder of Action for Sobriety Groups, President of Quotidian, and the mother of three adult children. Her three cats are of varied sizes.

REBECCA D. CHAITIN

Becca is a writer and editor, part-time alcoholism counselor and recovering alcoholic. Born in Virginia, she is a graduate of Hollins College and worked for various New York publishers, including Time-Life Books, before she began free-lancing in the early 1970's. She now lives in Montclair, New Jersey with her three teenagers and three immense cats.

GIFTS OF GROWTH

also come at

discount when ordering

in quantity

QUOTIDIAN

The word means "recurring daily". (One day at a time!) The thistle symbolizes the disease of alcoholism: the sharp leaves are the active illness; the flower is the beauty of recovery. The flower is an amethyst (purple) color. The Greeks believed the amethyst could protect one from drunkenness -- perhaps their idea of an easier, softer way?

QUOTIDIAN welcomes manuscripts (include SASE) on any aspect of alcoholism or personal growth.

PHONE NUMBERS

PHONE NUMBERS